Contents

Be a Treasure Hunter

People find many treasures on coasts around the world. You might find shells and colourful fishing floats, creatures from the deep sea or even jewels and coins from ancient shipwrecks!

What you can find

Waves wash all sorts of things from the sea on to the coast. Some treasures have travelled thousands of kilometres. **Cargo** washed ashore from wrecked ships can include anything from MP3 players to motorbikes. Animals also wash ashore. In 2007, a squid as long as a bus washed up on an Australian beach!

You can find amazing animals, such as enormous whales, washed up on beaches.

Coastal Kit

To treasure hunt, you must take a basic kit with you. You need:

* small trowel
* plastic bags
* clear plastic bucket
* **identification guides**
* gloves
* notebook, pencil, and sketchpad
* bottle of drinking water and snacks or packed lunch
* suncream and sun hat

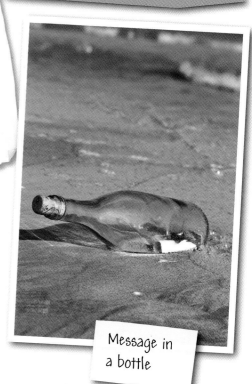

DANGER!

Stay alert for dangerous finds! In 2008, a huge World War II German mine washed up on a beach in Somerset, UK. It had to be exploded at sea by bomb disposal experts.

Message in a bottle

Beautiful shells

Explorer code

If you see anything on a beach that you suspect is dangerous, don't touch it, keep well away and call the coastguard on 999.

Be Prepared

To be a coastal treasure hunter you must plan ahead and be prepared. Before you set out, you should check the tides and the weather.

Check the weather forecast

The weather can change quickly at the coast. Find the weather forecast in a local newspaper, on the radio, television, or Internet. If storms are forecast, stay at home.

Coastal Kit

Use the weather forecast to help you decide what to wear.

* If it is going to be hot and sunny, wear a hat and put on suncream.
* If it is going to be wet and cold, wear warm jumpers and waterproofs.

High tide is not a good time to hunt for treasure.

It's best to treasure hunt in sturdy footwear, such as boots.

Check the tides

Before you go to a beach, check the times of high and low tide. High tide is when the sea rises up the beach. Low tide is when it has gone out again. Go after high tide to find new treasures washed in by the water. To find tide times:

1. Type www.bbc.co.uk/weather/coast/tides into your Internet search box.
2. Click on "Tide Tables".
3. Click on the region where you live.
4. Click on your nearest port.
5. Look at the table that tells you what time (in 24-hour clock) high tide happens.

Look out for danger signs.

Do not try treasure hunting in rough weather.

Know Your Coasts

To succeed on a beach treasure hunt, it helps
to know about different kinds of coasts. Coasts
are shaped by the power of the sea's waves.

Headlands

Headlands form when waves **erode** the soft rock on either side of a
lump of hard rock, which is left jutting out into the sea. Headlands
are great places to see huge groups of nesting seabirds,
like comical puffins or elegant shearwaters. Be
warned, bird colonies are very noisy and
their guano (droppings) can
stink on a hot day!

Seabirds, such as these guillemots,
can often be seen on headlands.

Estuaries

Estuaries are areas of coast where rivers run into the sea. Muddy estuaries are the places to hunt for animals like secretive razorshells. These animals live in long, thin shells but burrow quickly into the mud when they feel footsteps coming! Watch out for greeny-purple ragworms – they have teeth and can bite!

Estuaries make great animal treasure hunting ground.

Sandy bays

Sandy bays are where waves have eroded a curve of soft rock, so they are sheltered spots. Here you can hunt for shiny beetles and stripy caterpillars on plants at the back of the beach, crabs scuttling across the sand, and seals resting by the water's edge.

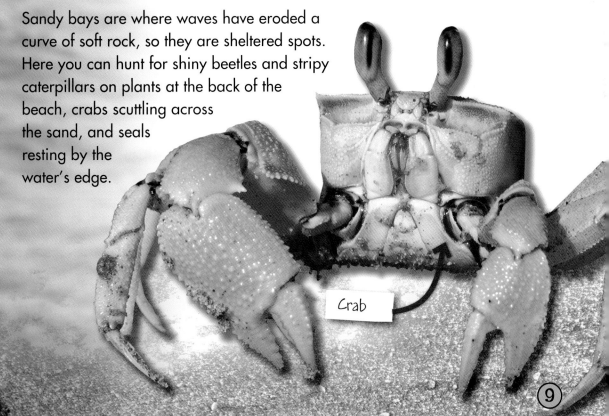

Crab

Finding Fossils

Go to cliffs to hunt for fossil treasures like sharks' teeth, trilobites, and ammonites. These exciting finds are the remains of animals that lived millions of years ago. You may not have to look very hard – the largest snail-like ammonite fossil ever found was as big as the tyre of a lorry!

How to find fossils

1. Check carefully under rocks, and move stones or boulders.

2. To find fossils inside a rock, put on the safety goggles and split the rock using a hammer and chisel.

3. Check what you find in your fossil guide.

4. Put fossils safely in your collecting bag.

5. If you find something special, take it to your nearest **Heritage Centre**.

Ammonite fossils formed millions of years ago.

Coastal kit

For fossil hunting take:

* fossil guide book
* geological hammer and chisel
* safety goggles
* collecting bag

Fossils are sometimes uncovered when part of the cliff falls into the sea.

If you are really lucky, you might find a dinosaur fossil, like this one!

Explorer code

Follow these rules when seeking treasure under cliffs.

* Read and obey any warning signs.
* Wear a protective hard hat under steep cliffs where rock falls may happen.
* Do not climb up cliffs.
* Find out the local rules about where you can search.

DANGER!

Do not go near the edge at the top of a cliff. Wind and waves erode cliff edges so they can crumble under your feet.

Pebble Treasures

Visit shingle beaches to find pebbles rubbed smooth by crashing against each other in the sea. Look closely and you may also find sea glass, or even gems like **jet** and **agate**.

How to identify common stones

Look for pebbles or stones that are interesting shapes or colours. Then use this list to work out what type of rock your pebble came from.

* Sandstone feels grainy because it is formed from colourful layers of sand.
* Limestone has lots of tiny shells in it.
* Granite looks speckled because it has different coloured **minerals** in it.
* Slate is grey and breaks into pieces easily.
* Flint has smooth surfaces and sharp edges.
* Rose quartz is pink and shiny.

Pebble treasure is great for making simple scultpures.

Sea glass

When pieces of glass are worn by waves they become sea glass. To find colourful sea glass, walk slowly across a beach and look carefully among the pebbles. Choose those with completely smooth edges.

THINGS TO MAKE

To make a paperweight, first find a smooth flat stone. At home, paint it with acrylic paint and leave it to dry. Then paint your name on the stone. When this dries, seal it by painting with varnish.

Sea glass

Beach diamonds

Amazing finds

At a beach in South Africa diamonds can be found all along the seafront and in the sea!

Seeking Shells

Sand consists of tiny pieces of stones and shells broken up by waves and **deposited** on the shore, but look closely and you may also find perfect, whole shells on beaches.

Where to find shells

To find shells, go to the coast at low tide and ideally after a storm. Look near boulders and rocks, where shells get jammed at the bottom or in cracks. To find bigger shells search higher parts of the beach and dig down in the top layer of sand to find buried shells.

These shells are called winkle shells.

Shells such as this one were once home to sea animals.

Razor shell

THINGS TO MAKE

Use glue to stick small magnets to large flat shells to make a simple fridge magnet. Use it to attach photos and notes to your fridge.

How to clean shells

Clean your seashells so they don't smell.

1. Put on gloves and ask for an adult's help.
2. Fill a bowl with half water and half bleach. (Don't get bleach on skin or clothes.)
3. Soak the shells until they look clean.
4. Rinse the shells in clean water.

Identify your shells

Put your shells into two categories: single-shelled and two-shelled (bivalves). Some bivalves may have lost one of their shells, so look for the place where the shell was once hinged to its other shell.

A fleshy animal called a scallop once lived in this shell.

Cowrie shell

15

Hunting in Mud

Estuaries are great places to find driftwood – wood smoothed and carved into amazing shapes by waves. There are also other treasures that you cannot take home, but only admire, such as strange animals that lurk beneath the surface of the mud and weird and wonderful plants.

Find animals in the mud

1. Scan the mud's surface for clues, like holes used by animals for breathing, bubbles of air or worm casts.
2. Use a spade to dig into the mud.
3. Count the snails, worms and other animals you find.
4. Take photos of interesting finds.
5. Put mud and animals back where they were.

This driftwood was once a tree.

Coastal kit

For estuary visits take:

* wellington boots
* a spade
* a camera

Worm casts are small piles of Earth left behind by a worm after it feeds.

Plants to look for

Estuary plants store freshwater for when the estuary fills with salty seawater that they cannot use. When looking for plants like these tread carefully. Look out for glasswort. This plant looks like a tiny, shiny cactus and it stores freshwater in its fat stems.

DANGER!

Do not walk into very wet, muddy areas because you might get stuck. Stay at the back of the beach where the mud is drier and harder.

Birds such as this curlew hunt for food in estuaries.

Rock Pools

Look out for fantastic wildlife treasure in rock pools. Don't forget to take your net to catch things with, and a camera for taking amazing photographs – then sit and wait for your treasure to appear!

Rock pool treasures

Go to the rocks at the water's edge at low tide. Rock pools are dips in rocks eroded by the waves that hold seawater at low tide. Look out for dark red blobs that look like jelly. These are sea anemones and they have tentacles that can reach out to sting tiny fish. Spot starfish too. Starfish have five legs with tiny suckers on to help them move in rock pools. If they lose a leg, they can grow a new one!

What do you think you might find in this rock pool?

Catch and snap

1 If nothing moves in the pool, gently brush a stick through the seaweed.

2 Turn rocks over gently, but make sure you replace them.

3 Catch small fish, shrimp, and other animals in a hand net. Put them in a clear plastic bucket filled with water. Then watch and photograph them.

4 Afterwards, release the animals into the same pool.

Blenny fish

Starfish

Sea anenome

Along the Strandline

The strandline is a mixture of seaweed, waste, and all sorts of treasures washed in by high tides.

Find and walk the strandline

1. Walk about halfway down the beach, between the top and the water, looking for a line of **debris**.

2. To check you are in the right place, feel if the sand is dry above the strandline and damp below.

3. Follow the strandline across the beach and turn over piles of seaweed or debris to see what lies beneath.

DANGER!

Watch out for old fish hooks that can give a nasty cut, bottles that may contain dangerous chemicals, and oil that can spoil clothing and stick to your hands.

Coconuts are sometimes washed up thousands of kilometres away from the tree they fell from.

Sort your treasures

Sort your finds into natural and synthetic.

* Natural finds include animal bones, egg cases, seed cases, and shells.

* Synthetic treasures include plastic fishing floats, painted wood panels from boats, nets, and bits of colourful rope.

Dolphin bones

Sea dragon

Amazing finds

Look carefully and you might find:

* a sea potato – a sea urchin that lives just below the surface of clean sand

* a mermaids purse – the dried, empty egg case of a dogfish or ray

* a sea dragon – seahorses that live among and look like seaweed.

At the Water's Edge

You need to wear wellington boots to explore the water's edge. Explore the seaweed that grows on the rocks and look for crabs and other animals that might be sheltering there.

Be a seaweed detective

Use this checklist to identify seaweeds. Keep a list or sketches of the ones you see.

* If it has bubbly air pockets along the **fronds**, it is bladderwrack.
* If it has bright green, flat, and slimy fronds it is sea lettuce.
* If it has long, very narrow fronds it is thongweed.
* If it has saw-like edges to the fronds, it is saw wrack.

Locate the names of other seaweeds you find in an identification guide.

This seaweed is called bladderwrack.

Spotting animals

1 Use a stick to lift seaweed gently.

2 Look first for crabs, because they burrow quickly under sand to hide from view.

3 Look on rocks to find barnacles and mussels. These creatures close their shells to stop drying out when the tide is low, and open them to feed when the tide comes in.

4 Look at seaweed closely to see snails such as periwinkles feeding on the fronds.

5 Do not remove animals. Take photos instead.

DANGER!

Never touch jellyfish washed up at the water's edge – some can still sting even when dead!

Jellyfish

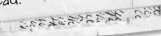

Two small creatures called barnacles are clinging to this shell.

Pirate Treasure!

Metal detecting to find treasure can be very exciting, especially after storms. Then, the waves have churned up sand and possibly washed up new items. Some treasure hunters find coins or other valuables at the coast, washed in from wrecked ships or dropped by visitors.

How to use a metal detector

1. Find an area of soft sand, just above the wet sand line.

2. Turn the metal detector on.

3. Walk slowly and in a straight line, sweeping the arm left and right across the sand.

4. Stop when the metal detector beeps.

5. Dig there, sifting through the sand carefully as you go (treasure can be small).

6. Place treasure safely in a bag and start again.

Wonderful treasures can be left behind by a ship wreck.

Explorer code

* If you find any really old or valuable treasure, report it.

* If an item is historically valuable, give it to a museum.

* If you find a suspicious object, like a metal canister, do not touch. Report it to the coastguard.

You may find real treasure just by looking carefully.

Metal detector

Amazing finds

In Anglesey, UK, two friends using a metal detector found more than 900 silver pennies that were over 600 years old!

Protect the Coast

Hunting for coastal treasure is great fun, but don't forget to look after the beaches while you are there. Here are some ideas for how you can help to protect the coast.

Dos and don'ts

* Join an organisation that protects beaches. The National Trust protects one in every five miles of UK coastline.

* Find out more about coasts so you can educate other people.

* Report any stranded or injured animal on a beach to the coastguard.

* Organise or join a beach clean-up, to clear waste from the coast.

* Never leave litter. Take it home with you or put it in a nearby bin.

* Do not disturb bird's nests by going too close.

You may even find treasure while clearing up the beach!

Look closely to see insects and small animals among sand dunes.

THINGS TO MAKE

Visit sand dunes early in the morning and take a tracker's guide to identify any animal footprints and droppings. Make a **plaster cast** of interesting footprints!

Sand dunes

Take special care with sand dunes. These rounded hills of sand form slowly from sand blown up the beach. Grass roots hold them together, but dunes are fragile. Do not walk on dune plants because if these are damaged, the dunes may erode.

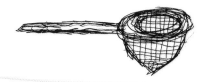

Coastguards can contact animal rescue teams to help any stranded animals found on the beach.

Make a Wind Chime

Follow these step-by-step instructions to make a set of wind chimes. Hang the chimes in your garden or give them as a gift.

How to make wind chimes

1. Take two pieces of driftwood about 20 cm (almost 8 in) long and put one on top of the other to form an "X" shape.

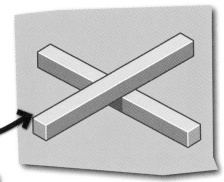

2. Use a piece of string to tie the driftwood sticks together at the point where they cross.

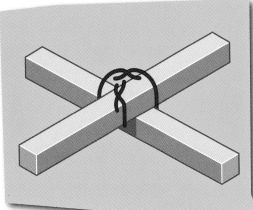

3. Leave one long, loose end of the string. You will use this to hang the wind chime up when it is finished.

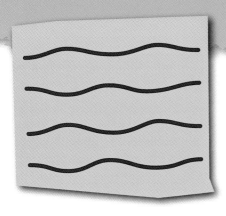

4. Cut four pieces of string, each about 60–80 cm (about 24–32 in) long.

5. Use sewing thread to tie shells, pebbles, junk, chunks of driftwood, and other seaside treasures along the length or each of the four long pieces of string. Take time to space the treasures in a way that looks interesting.

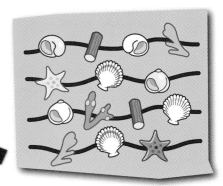

6. Tie one end of each of the four long pieces of string to the four ends of the driftwood "X".

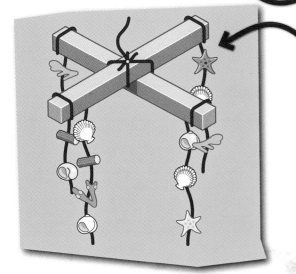

7. Make a loop with the loose end of string above the driftwood "X" and use this to hang your wind chimes from a hook in a porch, window, or garden.

Glossary

agate a kind of quartz stone in which the colours are in bands or swirls

cargo goods carried by a large vehicle, such as a ship

debris pieces of waste that are left somewhere, like on a coast

deposit to leave or drop something. Waves washing on to a coast may deposit sand or waste there.

erode when rocks or other things are worn away by the action of the wind, ice, rain, or waves

frond a long piece of seaweed that looks like a leaf

Heritage Centre a museum that presents historical and other local information about a particular place and its people

identification guide a book with pictures and descriptions of a particular type of thing, which people use to find out the names and other information

jet a hard black substance used for making jewellery

minerals non-living substances found naturally in the Earth, such as gold or quartz

plaster cast a copy of something made from plaster

Further Information

Websites

Find out more about protecting coasts at the Marine Conservation Society website:

www.mcsuk.org

Find out more information about coasts at:

www.bbc.co.uk/schools/riversandcoasts

There is a shell identification guide at:

www.seashells.org/seashells/sanibelseashellident.htm

Books

Coasts (Young Explorer: My World of Geography) by Vicky Parker. Heinemann Library (2005).

Coasts (Mapping Earthforms) by Melanie Waldron and Nicholas Lapthorn. Heinemann Library (2007).

The World's Most Amazing Coasts (Landform Top Tens) by Anna Claybourne, Michael Hurley and Anita Ganeri. Raintree (2009).

Index